Our Magnificent Men
in their Flying Machines

Written by David Forsyth

CD tracks:
1. The Best Is Yet to Come
2. Let's Do It (with Eddi Reader)
3. Autumn in New York (with Carol Kidd)
4. My Favorite Things
5. They Can't Take That Away from Me
6. Medley

©2012. Published by Pillar Box Red Publishing Ltd., Edinburgh. Printed in China

The CD attached to this book is a sampler from the new album by the Royal Air Force Squadronaires & Todd Gordon, licensed from Audacious Music Ltd. All profits from this album will be donated to Help for Heroes. Every effort has been made to ensure the accuracy of information within this publication but the publishers cannot be held responsible for any errors or omissions. Views expressed are those of the author and do not necessarily represent those of the publisher.

ISBN 978-1-907823-473

Contents

CHAPTER 1
Through Adversity to the Stars

The Royal Air Force is one of the biggest and most capable air forces in the world. With more than 800 aircraft and 41,000 active personnel, it is the biggest air force in the European Union, and of the NATO countries, only the US Air Force is larger.

The RAF's own mission says it exists to provide, "an agile, adaptable and capable Air Force that, person for person, is second to none." Now, equipped with supersonic jet aircraft, sophisticated helicopters and smart technology weaponry, the service more than matches its mission.

While most of the aircraft are based in the UK, others are deployed around the world, representing British interests in places as far flung as Afghanistan and the Middle East, or at long established bases in Cyprus, Ascension Island, Gibraltar and the Falklands.

As recently as 2011, RAF crews played a key role in the international effort to create and police a "no-fly" zone over Libya, where the people staged an ultimately successful uprising against Colonel Gaddafi.

And of course, in the decades since the end of WW2, the RAF has served with great distinction in various theatres including Korea, the Falklands, The Gulf War, the war in Iraq and in Afghanistan.

The RAF grew out of The Royal Flying Corps which came into existence in April 1912, as the potential to use aircraft for observation was recognised by the military. King George V signed a royal warrant establishing the Corps, with its two main operational wings being the Military wing – the Army wing which was originally the Air Battalion of the Royal Engineers – and a Naval wing run by the Royal Navy.

The original strength was 133 officers, and by the end of 1912 the Corps had 12 manned balloons and 36 aeroplanes. The motto – *Per Ardua Ad Astra* – means, "Through adversity to the stars", and remains the motto of the Royal Air Force to this day.

Flying was still very much in its infancy, and it didn't take long for the Royal Flying Corps

"The RAF grew out of The Royal Flying Corps which came into existence in April 1912, as the potential to use aircraft for observation was recognised by the military."

to suffer its first loss. On July 5th 1912, near Stonehenge, Captain Eustace Loraine and his observer, Staff Sergeant RHV Wilson, were killed when flying from Larkhill Aerodrome. An order was issued after the crash, stating, "Flying will continue this evening as usual", beginning a tradition which remains.

Expansion was inevitable, but the dawning of the First World War accelerated matters. That same year, 1914, the Naval Wing of the RFC broke away to establish the Royal Naval Air Service. The remaining RFC was also significantly expanded. When the RFC deployed to France it sent four squadrons, each with 12 aircraft. Further aircraft in depots gave a total strength of 63 aircraft, supported by 900 men. By September 1915 the strength stood at 12 squadrons and 161 aircraft.

For much of this time, observation provided the key role for all aircraft – planes and static balloons were used to undertake reconnaissance and artillery observation. The technology of arming aircraft was crude – weapons had to be fired without hitting the plane's propeller or wing struts – and for the early part of the war, injuries and deaths were largely the result of flying accidents.

Nonetheless, there were losses. Pilots were shot down by infantry fire and faced danger each time they took to the skies. Sir John French, the commander of the British Expeditionary Force in France, commended, "the admirable work done by the Royal Flying Corps." He said: "Their skill, energy and perseverance have been beyond all

Winning the War From the Clouds

praise. They have furnished me with most complete and accurate information which has been of incalculable value in the conduct of operations. Fired at constantly by friend and foe alike, and not hesitating to fly in every kind of weather, they have remained undaunted throughout. Further, by actually flying in the air they have succeeded in destroying five of the enemy's machines."

But as armament technology improved, so the danger to aircrew increased markedly. By the end of the war, one in four aircrew was killed, a similar proportion to the slaughter in the trenches. For much of the time, the RFC were up against an enemy that was superior in terms of numbers and the quality of its aircraft. British losses were four for every one suffered by Germany.

The first major air action took place over the Battle of the Somme in 1916. Hugh Trenchard, then in command in France, adopted a much more aggressive approach, in particular developing the strategy of using air power to support ground troops.

By the end of the war, the RFC deployed some 1200 aircraft in France, with further aircraft deployed in Britain as air defence against Zeppelin raids.

The Royal Air Force can trace its roots to the summer of 1917 when German bombers mounted raids over London and South African General Jan Smuts was invited by the Imperial War Cabinet, on which he served, to examine the air defence of Great Britain.

The RAF was founded in April 1918 through the amalgamation of the Royal Flying Corps and the Royal Naval Air Service, and was controlled by the newly formed British Government Air Ministry.

The newly created RAF was the world's first independent air force, free of control by either Army or Navy. It had more than 20,000 aircraft and more than 300,000 personnel.

After the conclusion of the First World War, the RAF was used to police the skies over Britain's fading Empire under Sir Hugh Trenchard, then Chief of the Air Staff, in particular in Somaliland and – as today – Afghanistan. During these inter-war years the RAF had to fight to maintain its

independence and a reorganisation saw the creation of three new Commands – Bomber Command, Fighter Command and Coastal Command – in 1936.

With the outbreak of World War Two, expansion accelerated, including the secondment of many whole squadrons and tens of thousands of men and women from Commonwealth air forces – in particular from Canada and Australia.

The main RAF effort in the war was the work of Bomber Command in which a total of 19 men were awarded the nation's highest award for gallantry, the Victoria Cross. The strategic bombing campaign waged against Germany often involved night time raids with up to 1,000 planes involved.

Fighter pilots also played a key role. In the summer of 1940, the role played by "The Few", as Prime Minister Sir Winston Churchill famously dubbed them, became known as The Battle of Britain. More accurately, it was a battle for Britain, with the courageous actions of the fighter pilots in holding off the Luftwaffe leading to the cancellation of Nazi Germany's "Operation Sea Lion" plans to invade Britain.

The Second World War also saw the development of iconic aircraft, in particular the Spitfire and Hurricane fighters and the Lancaster bomber, which were to play pivotal roles in winning the war.

Since the end of World War Two, the RAF has continued to see active service in theatres around the globe – most notably in the Falklands, the Gulf War, and more recently in Iraq and Afghanistan, as well as taking part in NATO operations in the Balkans.

Hugh Montague Trenchard has been described as the Father of the Royal Air Force. It was a title he personally demurred from, instead modestly insisting that the honour belonged to his own mentor, Lt Gen Sir David Henderson.

That both of these men deserve the accolade is beyond question. They stand head and shoulders above their contemporaries as the driving influence in shaping Britain's flying forces.

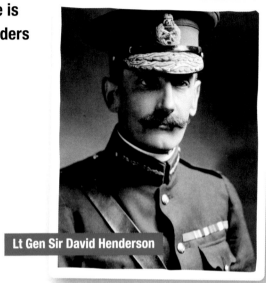

Lt Gen Sir David Henderson

David Henderson was born into a wealthy Glasgow shipping family and joined the Army after training at Sandhurst. He was a member of the Nile Expedition of 1898 and was wounded during the Boer War. In 1901 he was appointed Director of Military Intelligence by Lord Kitchener and quickly established his reputation as the Army's leading authority on tactical intelligence.

He learned to fly in 1911 at the age 49, making him the oldest pilot in the world at the time. He was part of the Air Committee which helped to decide upon the organisation of the Royal Flying Corps in 1912, and was then appointed Director of the new Department of Military Aeronautics. At the outbreak of WW1 Henderson was given command of the Royal Flying Corps in the Field.

In 1915 he returned to London to resume his post with Military Aeronautics, and worked closely with General Jan Smuts in his report into the state of Britain's Air Defence.

His son, Ian, also joined the RFC, achieving the rank of Captain. He died in a flying accident in 1918.

After the end of the War, Henderson served as a military counsellor during the Paris Peace Conference until the signing of the Versailles Treaty in June 1919. He then became Director-General of the League of Red Cross Societies, based in Geneva in Switzerland, where he died in 1921, aged just 59.

Hugh Trenchard took over from Henderson as Commander of the RFC in the Field in France in 1915.

Born in Somerset in 1873, he had been a military man since joining the army in 1893 and took part in the Boer War, suffering a severe lung wound in the process. He learned to fly in 1912 at the Sopwith Flying School.

During World War One he was appointed to head the Royal Flying Corps in Britain, before taking over from Henderson in France in 1915.

His time in command saw three major priorities: support for and co-ordination with ground forces; a belief in the importance of taking a more aggressive, offensive approach to the use of air power; and finally, he believed the presence of aircraft in the skies played an important role in boosting morale.

He hit upon the strategy of launching successive waves of attacks to gain air control – a tactic which quickly became standard policy but also attracted criticism for the levels of losses incurred.

He was much admired by then Commander-in-Chief Sir Douglas Haig and was appointed as the first Chief of Air Staff in January 1918 but resigned shortly afterwards following a row with Air Minister Lord Rothermere. He was reappointed to the role the following year by Winston Churchill, and remained in this post until 1927 when he became the First Marshall of the RAF, the service's highest rank.

It was during this period between the wars that Trenchard oversaw many of the building blocks that would underpin RAF operations for years to come. The RAF College at Cranwell was founded, the world's first military air academy. The Aircraft Apprentice Scheme was set up to help provide and train specialist ground crew, and the RAF Staff College at Andover was established.

In 1930, Trenchard became Commissioner of the Metropolitan Police, serving until 1935. He was knighted in 1918, created a Baronet in 1919 and a Viscount in 1930.

During the Second World War he turned down several roles he felt either required the services of a younger man, or that he felt did not suit his own strengths and talents, but as a friend of Winston Churchill he became a champion of the RAF's cause in the House of Lords and visited Air Force bases to boost morale.

During the war, tragedy visited his family: his stepson John was killed in action in Italy, his younger stepson Edward in a flying accident and his own older son Hugh was killed in North Africa. Trenchard's younger son, Thomas, survived the war.

Trenchard never liked the soubriquet of "Father of the Royal Air Force", believing that Sir David Henderson deserved the title. What is clear is that both men laid the foundations for a service now recognised for its excellence and for the courage and skill of its servicemen and women throughout the world.

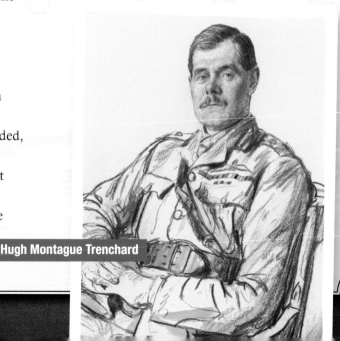

Hugh Montague Trenchard

CHAPTER 2
WWI Heroes

They were the young men whose pioneering courage paved the way for all of the combat pilots who were to follow in reconnaissance, fighters and in bombers. These magnificent men in their flying machines were courageous not only in that they flew in the face of enemy fire and attack – but that they flew at all!

The pilots who took to the skies over the bloody fields of France during the First World War did so at a time when flying was still in its infancy, when every flight was fraught with potential danger.

Yet fly they did, often in atrocious weather, in unsophisticated machines, and often locked in deadly combat with other pilots or even when being fired upon and shot down by ground troops.

Here we remember the deeds of some of the men who won their country's highest award for gallantry in the face of the enemy – The Victoria Cross – during the First World War.

William Barnard Rhodes-Moorhouse, RFC

The first VC awarded to a member of Britain's air services was announced in the London Gazette on May 22nd, 1915. The recipient was 2nd Lieutenant William Barnard Rhodes-Moorhouse, Special Reserve, Royal Flying Corps.

The London Gazette reported:

The London Gazette
Published by Authority

For most conspicuous bravery on 26th April, 1915, in flying to Courtrai and dropping bombs on the railway line near that station. On starting the return journey he was mortally wounded, but succeeded in flying for 35 miles to his destination, at a very low altitude, and reported the successful accomplishment of his object. He has since died of his wounds.

William Avery Bishop, RFC

In the summer of 1917 Captain William Avery Bishop, Canadian Cavalry and Royal Flying Corps, was flying alone over an enemy aerodrome twelve miles behind the lines, when he attacked seven machines which were on the ground.

The London Gazette of August 11th, 1917 said:

The London Gazette
Published by Authority

One of the machines got off the ground, but at a height of sixty feet Captain Bishop fired fifteen rounds into it at very close range, and it crashed to the ground.

A second machine got off the ground, into which he fired thirty rounds at 150 yards range, and it fell into a tree. Two more machines then rose from the aerodrome. One of these he engaged at the height of 1,000 feet, emptying the rest of his drum of ammunition. This machine crashed 300 yards from the aerodrome, after which Captain Bishop emptied a whole drum into the fourth hostile machine, and then flew back to his station.

Major Bishop transferred to the newly formed Royal Canadian Air Force after the war, and eventually retired as an Air Vice-Marshal.

William George Barker, RAF

Major William Barker was one of the most decorated men in the First World War, winning a number of his country's awards for gallantry – including the Military Cross and two bars, and the Distinguished Service Order and bar.

But it was action on the morning of October 27th, 1918, that saw him win the highest award, the Victoria Cross.

After spotting an enemy two-seater over the Foret de Mormal he attacked and shot down the enemy, but was himself attacked by a Fokker biplane and wounded in the right thigh. Despite his injury, he managed to shoot down the biplane also.

The London Gazette of November 30th, 1918, took up his story:

The London Gazette
𝕻ublished by 𝕬uthority

He then found himself in the middle of a large formation of Fokkers, who attacked him from all directions; and was again severely wounded in the left thigh; but succeeded in driving down two of the enemy in a spin. He lost consciousness after this, and his machine fell out of control. On recovery he found himself being again attacked heavily by a large formation, and singling out one machine, he deliberately charged and drove it down in flames.

During this fight his left elbow was shattered and he again fainted, and on regaining consciousness he found himself still being attacked, but, notwithstanding that he was now severely wounded in both legs and his left arm shattered, he dived on the nearest machine and shot it down in flames. Being greatly exhausted, he dived out of the fight to regain our lines, but was met by another formation, which attacked and endeavoured to cut him off, but after a hard fight he succeeded in breaking up this formation and reached our lines, where he crashed on landing.

This combat, in which Major Barker destroyed four enemy machines (three of them in flames), brought his total successes up to fifty enemy machines destroyed, and is a notable example of the exceptional bravery and disregard of danger which this very gallant officer has always displayed throughout his distinguished career.

Albert Ball, RFC

Captain Albert Ball was a genuine fighter ace, a man who was eventually credited with bringing down 44 enemy aircraft.

He was awarded the Victoria Cross in May, 1917, in combat. His citation in June 1917 talked of his *"most conspicuous and consistent bravery"* during April and May 1917, when he took part in twenty-six combats in the air and destroyed eleven hostile aeroplanes, drove down two out of control, and forced several others to land.

Reginald Alexander John Warneford, RNAS

Flight Sub-Lieutenant Reginald Alexander John Warneford attacked and single-handedly destroyed a Zeppelin in mid-air on June 7th, 1915.

The Gazette of June 10th, 1915, reported:

The London Gazette
Published by Authority

This brilliant achievement was accomplished after chasing the Zeppelin from the coast of Flanders to Ghent, where he succeeded in dropping his bombs on to it from a height of only one or two hundred feet. One of these bombs caused a terrific explosion which set the Zeppelin on fire from end to end, but at the same time overturned his Aeroplane and stopped the engine. In spite of this he succeeded in landing safely in hostile country, and after 15 minutes started his engine and returned to his base without damage.

Alan Jerrard, RAF

Lieutenant Alan Jerrard was on an offensive patrol with two other officers in Spring 1918 when he attacked five enemy aeroplanes.

He shot one down in flames, following it to within one hundred feet of the ground, before attacking an enemy aerodrome from a height of only fifty feet.

He set about attacking 19 enemy machines which were either landing or attempting to take off, and succeeded in destroying one of them, which crashed on the aerodrome. A large number of machines then attacked him.

The citation for his Victoria Cross, published in the London Gazette of May 1st, 1918, took up his tale:

The London Gazette
Published by Authority

He observed that one of the pilots of his patrol was in difficulties. He went immediately to his assistance, regardless of his own personal safety, and destroyed a third enemy machine.

Fresh enemy aeroplanes continued to rise from the aerodrome, which he attacked one after another, and only retreated, still engaged with five enemy machines, when ordered to do so by his patrol leader. Although apparently wounded, this very gallant officer turned repeatedly, and attacked single-handed the pursuing machines, until he was eventually overwhelmed by numbers and driven to the ground. Lt. Jerrard had greatly distinguished himself on four previous occasions, within a period of twenty-three days, in destroying enemy machines, displaying bravery and ability of the very highest order.

John Aidan Liddell, RFC

Captain John Aidan Liddell demonstrated the most conspicuous bravery and devotion to duty whilst flying on reconnaissance over Ostend-Bruges-Ghent on 31st July, 1915.

His plane fell by almost 3,000 feet after he was severely wounded – his right thigh was broken – which caused a momentary loss of consciousness.

However, through a tremendous effort he recovered control of his machine and, notwithstanding his injuries and the fact that he was still under fire, succeeded in returning his aeroplane to British lines.

The London Gazette reported on August 23rd, 1915:

The London Gazette
Published by Authority

The difficulties experienced by this Officer in saving his machine, and the life of his observer, cannot be readily expressed, but as the control wheel and throttle control were smashed, and also one of the undercarriage struts, it would seem incredible that he could have accomplished his task.

Gilbert Stuart Martin Insall, RFC

Second Lieutenant Gilbert Insall showed skill, courage and determination in combat with the enemy on 7th November, 1915, in France while patrolling in a Vickers Fighting Machine with his gunner, First Class Air Mechanic T. H. Donald.

After they spotted a German machine near Achiet, they pursued and attacked. The German pilot led the Vickers machine over a rocket battery.

The London Gazette

Published by Authority

With great skill Lieutenant Insall dived and got to close range, when Donald fired a drum of cartridges into the German machine, stopping its engine. The German pilot then dived through a cloud, followed by Lieutenant Insall. Fire was again opened, and the German machine was brought down heavily in a ploughed field four miles south-east of Arras.

On seeing the Germans scramble out of their machine and prepare to fire, Lieutenant Insall dived to 500 feet, thus enabling Donald to open heavy fire on them. The Germans then fled, one helping the other, who was apparently wounded. Other Germans then commenced heavy fire, but in spite of this, Lieutenant Insall turned again, and an incendiary bomb was dropped on the German machine, which was last seen wreathed in smoke. Lieutenant Insall then headed west in order to get back over the German trenches, but as he was at only 2,000 feet altitude he dived across them for greater speed, Donald firing into the trenches as he passed over.

The Vickers' petrol tank had been damaged in the action, but coolly Lieutenant Insall landed 500 yards inside British lines. His plane had been badly damaged by rifle fire, but during the night it was repaired, and at dawn Lieutenant Insall flew his machine home. He was awarded the Victoria Cross.

Edward Mannock, RAF

Major Edward Mannock was one of the most distinguished and decorated fliers of the war, accounting for the destruction of 50 enemy machines and repeatedly gaining honours for his courage in the face of the enemy.

He won his Victoria Cross – having already been awarded the Military Cross and Bar, and Distinguished Service Order and two Bars – for bravery of the first order shown in aerial combat in June and July of 1918.

On the 17th June, he attacked a Halberstadt machine near Armentieres and destroyed it from a height of 8,000 feet. On the 7th July, he destroyed one Fokker and attacked another biplane, firing 60 rounds into it, forcing it to crash.

The London Gazette

Published by Authority

This highly distinguished officer, during the whole of his career in the Royal Air Force, was an outstanding example of fearless courage, remarkable skill, devotion to duty and self-sacrifice, which has never been surpassed. The total number of machines definitely accounted for by Major Mannock up to the date of his death in France (26th July, 1918) is fifty.

On the 14th July, he attacked and crashed a Fokker from 7,000 feet, and brought a two-seater down damaged. The next day, he fired 80 rounds into an Albatross two-seater, which went to the ground in flames. A day later, he attacked and crashed an enemy two-seater from a height of 10,000 feet. About an hour afterwards he attacked at 8,000 feet a Fokker biplane near Steenwercke and drove it down out of control.

Finally, on the 22nd July, he destroyed an enemy triplane.

Alan Arnett McLeod, RAF

Canadian Lieutenant Alan Arnett McLeod was flying with his observer, Lieutenant A.W. Hammond, in March 1918, when they were attacked by eight enemy triplanes.

Through their own skill and courage, the pair tackled the attacking pack, shooting three of them down. Lt McLeod had received five wounds but continued to fight when a bullet hit his petrol tank and set the machine on fire.

The London Gazette reported:

The London Gazette
Published by Authority

He then climbed out on to the left bottom plane, controlling his machine from the side of the fuselage, and by side-slipping steeply kept the flames to one side, thus enabling the observer to continue firing until the ground was reached.

The observer had been wounded six times when the machine crashed in "No Man's Land," and

2nd Lt McLeod, notwithstanding his own wounds, dragged him away from the burning wreckage at great personal risk from heavy machine-gun fire from the enemy's lines. This very gallant pilot was again wounded by a bomb whilst engaged in this act of rescue, but he persevered until he had placed Lt Hammond in comparative safety, before falling himself from exhaustion and loss of blood.

Lt McLeod was returned home to recuperate from his wounds, but sadly died of Spanish 'flu soon afterwards.

Thomas Mottershead, RFC

Thomas Mottershead was awarded the Victoria Cross, the London Gazette reported on February 12ᵗʰ, 1917, for *"most conspicuous bravery, endurance and skill."*

Sergeant Mottershead was flying at an altitude of 9,000 feet when his plane was attacked. The petrol tank was pierced and the machine set on fire. The observer was unable to subdue the flames, which enveloped the plane, but Mottershead somehow succeeded in bringing his aeroplane back to the British line.

Although he made a successful landing, the machine collapsed on touching the ground, pinning him beneath wreckage from which he was subsequently rescued.

The Gazette said:

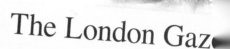

The London Gaz

Published by Authority

Though suffering extreme torture burns, Sgt. Mottershead showed s[...] the most conspicuous presence of [...] in the careful selection of a landing [...] and his wonderful endurance and fort[...] undoubtedly saved the life of his obse[...] He has since succumbed to his injuries.

The London Gazette

Published by Authority

Early in the duel one of his legs was partially severed by an explosive bullet, and fell powerless into the controls, rendering the machine for the time unmanageable. Lifting his disabled leg, he regained control of the machine, and, although wounded in the other leg, he, with surpassing bravery and devotion to duty, manoeuvred his machine so skilfully that his observer was enabled to get several good bursts into the enemy machines, which drove them away. Captain West then, with rare courage, and determination, desperately wounded as he was, brought his machine over our lines and landed safely. Exhausted by his exertions, he fainted, but on regaining consciousness insisted on writing his report.

Ferdinand Maurice Felix West, RAF

An extraordinary tale of courage was told in November 1918, when the Air Ministry announced in the London Gazette the award of the Victoria Cross to acting Captain Ferdinand Maurice Felix West, in recognition of his outstanding bravery in aerial combat.

While engaging hostile troops at a low altitude far over the enemy lines, he was attacked by seven aircraft.

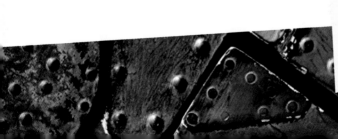

James Byford McCudden, RFC

At the time his award was announced in the London Gazette in April 1918, Captain McCudden accounted for 54 enemy aeroplanes – having destroyed 42 and driven a further twelve out of control.

On two occasions, he destroyed four two-seater enemy aeroplanes on the same day. With his squadron he took part in 78 offensive patrols, in nearly every case as the leader. On at least 30 other occasions, whilst with the same squadron, he crossed the lines alone, either in pursuit or in quest of enemy aeroplanes.

The Gazette stated:

The London Gazette

Published by Authority

As a patrol leader he has at all times shown the utmost gallantry and skill, not only in the manner in which he has attacked and destroyed the enemy, but in the way he has during several aerial fights protected the newer members of his flight, thus keeping down their casualties to a minimum.

This officer is considered, by the record, which he has made, by his fearlessness, and by the great service which he has rendered to his country, deserving of the very highest honour.

Captain McCudden died on 9th July, 1918, in a flying accident as he took off in a SE5A to take over command of No 56 Squadron.

The daring of the young pilots who took on the might of the German air force captured the imagination of the people back at home – but it also reinforced the need to accelerate the development of better aircraft. Here are some of the iconic planes that took to the skies during the Great War, including two fighters that helped to turn the tide in the air.

Vickers F.B.5

The **Vickers F.B.5** (Fighting Biplane 5) was known as the "Gunbus". It was a British two-seater, armed with a single Lewis Gun operated by the observer. It was the first aircraft purpose-built for air-to-air combat to see service, making it the world's first operational fighter aircraft.

Production of the **Avro 504** biplane during the war totalled 8,970 and continued for almost 20 years, making it the most-produced aircraft of any kind that served in World War One, in any military capacity throughout the conflict.

Avro 504

Sopwith Camel

The legendary **Sopwith Camel** was a single-seat biplane fighter introduced on the Western Front in 1917. It concentrated fire from twin synchronized machine guns and, to an experienced pilot, it provided unmatched manoeuvrability. The Camel was credited with shooting down 1,294 enemy aircraft, more than any other Allied fighter of the war.

The **Royal Aircraft Factory S.E.5** biplane reached the Western Front before the Sopwith Camel and while it had a much better overall performance, problems with its engine meant that there was a shortage of S.E.5s until well into 1918. As such, fewer squadrons were equipped with it. Together with the Sopwith Camel, the S.E.5 was instrumental in regaining allied air superiority from mid-1917.

Royal Aircraft Factory S.E.5

CHAPTER 3
Bomber Command

Bombing was becoming fully established as a tactic in waging war by the end of the First World War. It was commonplace on or beyond the front lines from 1917 onwards. Germany had even launched raids on the British mainland by Zeppelin airship, and by bomber aircraft over London.

That led to a re-think in the way the RAF was structured. In 1936, as part of expansion plans in anticipation of World War Two, the RAF was split into four commands: Fighter, Bomber, Coastal and Training Command. New aircraft were developed and aircrews were recruited and trained.

While the fearless exploits of Britain's daring fighter pilots in the Battle of Britain captured the imagination and the headlines, it was the ceaseless and courageous work carried out by the men of Bomber Command which played, perhaps, the most significant role in defeating Nazi Germany.

From the start of the war until its end, Bomber Command's job was to fly night and day over enemy territory attacking its airbases, shipping, troops, communications and – vitally – the heavy industries of war. The aim was to damage or destroy the fabric which underpinned the German war effort, to damage civilian morale within Germany, and to tie up German men and machines in defending their territory.

In his speech to Parliament in August 1940 Winston Churchill praised "The Few" – the Battle of Britain fighter pilots. However it is often forgotten that Prime Minister also paid this glowing tribute to Bomber Command:

We must never forget that all the time, night after night, month after month, our bomber squadrons travel far into Germany, find their targets in the darkness by the highest navigational skill, aim their attacks, often under the heaviest fire, often with serious loss, with deliberate careful discrimination, and inflict shattering blows upon the whole of the technical and war-making structure of the Nazi power.

On no part of the Royal Air Force does the weight of the war fall more heavily than on the daylight bombers who will play an invaluable part in the case of invasion and whose unflinching zeal it has been necessary in the meanwhile on numerous occasions to restrain.

It has to be remembered that after the British Army's retreat across the Channel from Dunkirk in 1940, and until D-day in 1944, it was Bomber Command who took the war to Germany by long-range bombing.

That vital task fell to aircrews with an average age of just 22. The youngest were scarcely 18 years old yet they faced some of the most terrifying ordeals of the war. Many showed unimaginable courage, and more than 20 Victoria Crosses were awarded to Bomber Command crew, while only one was awarded to a fighter pilot during the Battle of Britain.

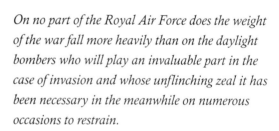

Bombing policy was a matter for politicians and the Air Ministry. Aerial bombing was seen as a preferable to the terrible loss of life suffered in the trenches in World War One. Churchill was a strong advocate of aerial bombing, realising the importance of forcing the Germans to defend their own homeland.

In September 1940, at the height of the Battle of Britain, he declared that the bombers alone "provide the means of victory."

Bomber Command was the only arm of the British forces to continually attack the German homeland throughout the war – and the casualty figures reflect that commitment, with 55,000 airmen killed.

However, in the early part of the war Bomber Command's raids had little effect. Daylight raids proved too costly in losses, and with poor navigation equipment on board it proved very difficult to locate specific small targets, like factories, in darkness. A new commander-in-chief of Bomber Command, Air Marshal Sir Arthur Harris was appointed. He was to achieve fame and notoriety as "Bomber" Harris.

Air Marshal Sir Arthur Harris

Harris, born in Cheltenham in 1892, had served in the Royal Flying Corps during the First World War before becoming a Squadron Leader in the newly formed RAF in 1918, serving in India and the Middle East.

At the time he took over as commander of Bomber Command, the combination of heavy losses of planes and men during daylight raids and inaccurate and ineffective night raids had led to the suspension of long-range raids by the RAF. To counter this, whole industrial cities were targeted in a tactic known as 'area bombing'. This was endorsed by Churchill and formally adopted in early 1942.

Although Harris followed through the city bombing campaign with dogged determination, he did not conceive the idea. Harris did not believe that city bombing would affect German morale, but he agreed that by destroying German industrial cities the Germans would eventually be unable to continue waging war.

In May 1942, he gathered together all of his available bombers and devastated Cologne in the first "thousand bomber" raid. Also, from early 1942, a new navigational aid allowed bombing on non-moonlit nights and helped guide the bombers onto the target. Also, more long-range four-engine bombers were becoming available, particularly the famous Avro Lancaster, which became the backbone of the Bomber Offensive.

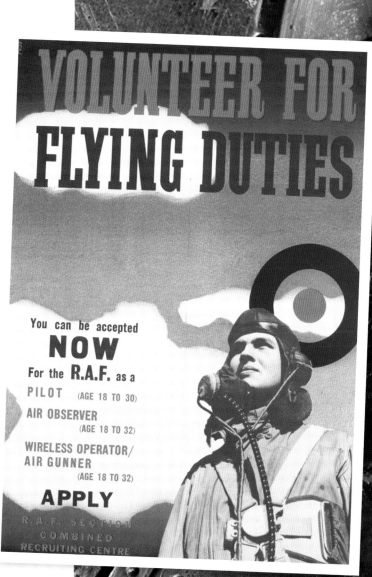

winning the war than he did. I doubt whether that is generally realised".

While Bomber Command is best known for its campaign against German industrial cities, its aircrews carried out many other types of mission.

From August 1942, the 'Pathfinders', began operating. Their task was to fly ahead of the other bombers and act as target-finders, locating the target and marking it with large coloured flares which the main force then aimed at. The Pathfinder's 'Master Bomber' would circle the target throughout the raid, sending instructions to the incoming bombers to ensure accuracy was maintained.

For three-and-a-half years Bomber Command pounded Germany, night after night.

During the war Harris was a household name, regarded as a great military leader who was hitting back at Germany. However, as the war came to an end and the level of destruction in Germany's cities became apparent, politicians distanced themselves from what had been inflicted on the enemy.

But according to the men and women who served under him, Sir Arthur Harris was a commander who won their respect, and also won it from the vast majority of his contemporaries including Churchill, Eisenhower and Montgomery, who said of Harris: "I doubt any single man did more in

For example, in 1940 during the British army's retreat to Dunkirk, airmen fought courageously to hold off the attacking German forces. Their planes were out-of-date, single-engine machines and few of the aircrews survived.

Blenheim bomber crews flew dangerous low-level daylight raids against shipping targets early in the war and suffered very high casualties. The British bombers also laid thousands of mines at sea, sinking hundreds of enemy ships throughout the war.

Precision raids were also carried out, and included bombing Hitler's V-rocket weapon development centre and the sinking of the 'Tirpitz' battleship. The Dambusters raid, covered in greater detail in Chapter Four, is perhaps the best known of the precision raids. In fact, despite the focus often placed on Bomber Command's role in city bombing, many successful precision raids took place across Europe. In one example, Bomber Command struck at a Berlin radio station as Goering, the Head of the Luftwaffe, began to broadcast a speech. This is particularly ironic, given that Goering had declared early in the war, "No enemy aircraft will fly over the Reich territory".

Advances in equipment, changes in tactics, and the development of better aircraft all played a key role in ensuring the success of Bomber Command. But it was the incredible courage and sacrifice shown by the aircrews themselves that helped turn the tide of the war. More than 20 individuals from Bomber Command were awarded their country's highest award for gallantry – the Victoria Cross. Here we look at a few examples of their bravery.

Sergeant John Hannah is the youngest recipient of the VC for aerial operations, showing incredible courage in tackling a fire on board his bomber – even using his bare hands in an attempt to beat out the flames.

He was just 18 years old when the following deed took place.

The London Gazette of Tuesday, October 1st, 1940, reported that Hannah was the wireless operator/air gunner on a bomber returning after a successful attack on enemy barges at Antwerp when the plane was hit in the bomb compartment by intense anti-aircraft fire and burst into flames.

The London Gazette

Published by Authority

A fire started which quickly enveloped the wireless operators and rear gunners' cockpits, and as both the port and starboard petrol tanks had been pierced, there was grave risk of the fire spreading. Sergeant Hannah forced his way through to obtain two extinguishers and discovered that the rear gunner had had to leave the aircraft. He could have acted likewise, through the bottom escape hatch or forward through the navigator's hatch, but remained and fought the fire for ten minutes with the extinguishers, beating the flames with his log book when these were empty.

During this time thousands of rounds of ammunition exploded in all directions and he was almost blinded by the intense heat and fumes, but had the presence of mind to obtain relief by turning on his oxygen supply. Air admitted through the large holes caused by the projectile made the bomb compartment an inferno and all the aluminium sheet metal on the floor of this airman's cockpit was melted away, leaving only the cross bearers.

Working under these conditions, which caused burns to his face and eyes, Sergeant Hannah succeeded in extinguishing the fire. He then crawled forward, ascertained that the navigator had left the aircraft, and passed the latter's log and maps to the pilot. This airman displayed courage, coolness and devotion to duty of the highest order and by his action in remaining and successfully extinguishing the fire under conditions of the greatest danger and difficulty, enabled the pilot to bring the aircraft to its base.

Sergeant Norman Jackson, the flight engineer on a Lancaster returning from a successful bombing mission, was called into extraordinary action in April 1944, high above Germany. Attacked by a German fighter, the plane's starboard wing was ablaze.

Wounded by shell splinters in his right leg and shoulder, he did something truly remarkable. He volunteered to try to put out the fire and obtained his Captain's permission to tackle the flames.

Tucking a hand fire extinguisher into his jacket and strapping on his parachute pack, he climbed out of the cockpit and made his way along the fuselage and onto the wing. It was bitterly cold. The plane was travelling at 200mph, 20,000 feet in the air.

The London Gazette of October 26th, 1945, told the story as follows:

Lancaster Bombers

The London Gazette
Published by Authority

Before he could leave the fuselage his parachute pack opened and the whole canopy and rigging lines spilled into the cockpit. Undeterred, Sergeant Jackson continued. The pilot (Tony Mifflin), bomb aimer (Maurice Toft) and navigator (Frank Higgins) gathered the parachute together and held on to the rigging lines, paying them out as the airman crawled aft. Eventually he slipped and, falling from the fuselage to the starboard wing, grasped an air intake on the leading edge of the wing. He succeeded in clinging on but lost the extinguisher, which was blown away.

By this time, the fire had spread rapidly and Sergeant Jackson was involved. His face, hands and clothing were severely burnt. Unable to retain his hold he was swept through the flames and over the trailing edge of the wing, dragging his parachute behind. When last seen it was only partly inflated and was burning in a number of places.

Realising that the fire could not be controlled, the captain gave the order to abandon aircraft. Four of the remaining members of the crew landed safely. The captain and rear gunner have not been accounted for.

Sergeant Jackson was unable to control his descent and landed heavily. He sustained a broken ankle, his right eye was closed through burns and his hands were useless. These injuries, together with the wounds received earlier, reduced him to a pitiable state. At daybreak he crawled to the nearest village, where he was taken prisoner. He bore the intense pain and discomfort of the journey to Dulag Luft with magnificent fortitude. After ten months in hospital he made a good recovery, though his hands require further treatment and are only of limited use.

This airman's attempt to extinguish the fire and save the aircraft and crew from falling into enemy hands was an act of outstanding gallantry. To venture outside, when travelling at 200 miles an hour, at a great height and in intense cold, was an almost incredible feat. Had he succeeded in subduing the flames, there was little or no prospect of his regaining the cockpit. The spilling of his parachute and the risk of grave damage to its canopy reduced his chances of survival to a minimum. By his ready willingness to face these dangers he set an example of self-sacrifice which will ever be remembered.

HE's doing his part

are YOU doing yours ?

He's wanted here AND NOW

39

George Thompson

Flight Sergeant **George Thompson** was 24 years old when the deed took place for which he was awarded the VC – the last RAF recipient of the award to date.

On 1st January, 1945, in an attack on the Dortmund-Ems Canal, Germany, the Lancaster bomber he was in had released its bombs when it was hit by two shells and a raging fire broke out. Flight Sergeant Thompson went through smoke and flame-filled fuselage not once, but twice, to rescue wounded comrades, suffering the most severe burns to his hands, legs and face. One of his comrades survived, the other died, and Flight Sergeant Thompson succumbed to his injuries three weeks later.

The London Gazette of February 20th, 1945, said:

The London Gazette

Published by Authority

This airman was the wireless operator in a Lancaster aircraft which attacked the Dortmund-Ems Canal in daylight on 1st January, 1945. The bombs had just been released when a heavy shell hit the aircraft in front of the mid-upper turret. Fire broke out and dense smoke filled the fuselage. The nose of the aircraft was then hit and an inrush of air, clearing the smoke, revealed a scene of utter devastation. Most of the perspex screen of the nose compartment had been shot away, gaping holes had been torn in the canopy above the pilot's head, the inter-communication wiring was severed, and there was a large hole in the floor of the aircraft. Bedding and other equipment were badly damaged or alight; one engine was on fire.

Flight Sergeant Thompson saw that the gunner was unconscious in the blazing mid-upper turret. Without hesitation he went down the fuselage into the fire and the exploding ammunition. He pulled the gunner from his turret and, edging his way round the hole in the floor, carried him away from the flames. With his bare hands, he extinguished the gunner's burning clothing. He himself sustained serious burns on his face, hands and legs.

Flight Sergeant Thompson then noticed that the rear gun turret was also on fire. Despite his own severe injuries he moved painfully to the rear of the fuselage where he found the rear gunner with his clothing alight, overcome by flames and fumes. A second time Flight Sergeant Thompson braved the flames. With great difficulty he extricated the helpless gunner and carried him clear. Again, he used his bare hands, already burnt, to beat out flames on a comrade's clothing.

Flight Sergeant Thompson, by now almost exhausted, felt that his duty was not yet done. He must report the fate of the crew to the captain. He made the perilous journey back through the burning fuselage, clinging to the sides with his burnt hands to get across the hole in the floor. The flow of cold air caused him intense pain and frost-bite developed. So pitiful was his condition that his captain failed to recognise him. Still, his only concern was for the two gunners he had left in the rear of the aircraft. He was given such attention as was possible until a crash-landing was made some forty minutes later.

When the aircraft was hit, Flight Sergeant Thompson might have devoted his efforts to quelling the fire and so have contributed to his own safety. He preferred to go through the fire to succour his comrades. He knew that he would then be in no position to hear or heed any order which might to given to abandon the aircraft. He hazarded his own life in order to save the lives of others. Young in years and experience, his actions were those of a veteran.

41

Flying Officer Leslie Thomas Manser was 20 years old when, on 30th May, 1942, he was captain and first pilot of an Avro Manchester bomber which took part in the first 1,000 bomber raid of the war, against Cologne.

He dropped his bombs successfully, but his aircraft was hit and the rear gunner was wounded. The front cabin filled with smoke and the port engine overheated. The plane lost altitude. Manser took the aircraft to 2,000 feet but then the port engine burst into flames. It was ten minutes before the fire was mastered. Part of one wing was burnt, and the air-speed of the plane became dangerously low.

Despite all the efforts of pilot and crew, the Manchester began to lose height. At this critical moment, Flying Officer Manser, with grim determination, set a new course for the nearest base. When the aircraft was over Belgium it became extremely difficult to handle and, when a crash was inevitable, Manser ordered the crew to bale out, refusing the offer of a parachute for himself. A sergeant handed him a parachute but he waved it away, telling the non-commissioned officer to jump at once as he could only hold the aircraft steady for a few seconds more. He remained at the controls and sacrificed himself in order to save his crew.

In October 1942, The London Gazette reported:

The London Gazette
Published by Authority

Flying Officer Manser was captain and first pilot of an aircraft which took part in the mass raid on Cologne on the night of 30th May, 1942. Despite searchlights and intense and accurate anti-aircraft fire he held his course and bombed the target successfully from 7,000 feet. Thereafter, although he took evasive action, the aircraft was badly damaged, for a time one engine and part of one wing were on fire, and in spite of all the efforts of pilot and crew, the machine became difficult to handle and lost height. Though he could still have parachuted to safety with his crew, he refused to do so and insisted on piloting the aircraft towards its base as long as he could hold it steady, to give his crew a better chance of safety when they jumped.

While the crew were descending to safety, they saw the aircraft, still carrying the gallant captain, plunge to earth and burst into flames. In pressing home his attack in the face of strong opposition, in striving against heavy odds to bring back his aircraft and crew, and finally, when in extreme peril, thinking only of the safety of his comrades, Flying Officer Manser displayed determination and valour of the highest order.

Bomber Command's first recipients of the Victoria Cross were Flying Officer Donald Garland and Sergeant Thomas Gray. Garland was pilot and Gray navigator in May 1940 on a single-engine Battle aircraft which led an attack on a bridge being used by the Nazis to advance into Belgium.

Thomas Gray

The five bombers that had flown on the mission were met with an inferno of anti-aircraft fire as well as enemy fighters in the skies, but the order had been given that the bridge was to be destroyed at all costs and all five planes dived through the hail of bullets and delivered their attack.

The London Gazette reported on June 11th, 1940:

The two men were 21 and 25 years old respectively.

The London Gazette
Published by Authority

Only one of the five aircraft concerned returned from this mission. The pilot of this aircraft reports that besides being subjected to extremely heavy anti-aircraft fire, through which they dived to attack the objective, our aircraft were also attacked by a large number of enemy fighters after they had released their bombs on the target. Much of the success of this vital operation must be attributed to the formation leader, Flying Officer Garland, and to the coolness and resource of Sergeant Gray, who in most difficult conditions navigated Flying Officer Garland's aircraft in such a manner that the whole formation was able successfully to attack the target in spite of subsequent heavy losses. Flying Officer Garland and Sergeant Gray did not return.

BE AN AIRMAN

APPLY TO THE NEAREST R.A.F. RECRUITING DEPOT
OR WRITE TO THE INSPECTOR OF RECRUITING
VICTORY HOUSE, KINGSWAY, LONDON W.C.2

THE HEROES

These are only examples of the courage shown by the airmen of Bomber Command in service of their country. The others to be awarded the Victoria Cross were:

Flight Lieutenant Roderick Learoyd, August 12th, 1940. Despite seeing all other aircraft in his raid which had gone in before him hit, Learoyd flew through fierce anti-aircraft fire at low altitude, attacked his target over the Dortmund-Ems Canal in Germany, and brought his crew and severely damaged aircraft back to base.

Wing Commander Hughie Edwards – despite being physically disadvantaged by an earlier accident – led his squadron on many low-level dangerous raids at great personal risk.

In an act of breathtaking heroism, **Sergeant James Ward** climbed out onto the wing of his Wellington bomber and extinguished a fire, thus saving his aircraft, which managed to return safely home after a raid on Munster in July 1941.

Squadron Leader John Nettleton led one of two formations of Lancasters on a daring and extremely dangerous low-level daylight raid to Augsburg, deep in Southern Germany, in April 1942. Successfully bombing despite appalling losses, his was the only aircraft to return.

Despite appalling injuries to his face, **Flight Sergeant Rawdon Middleton** flew his Stirling bomber back over the Alps after a raid on Turin in 1942. His actions allowed most of his crew to bale out over England before he crashed into the sea.

In December 1942, knowing his raid was vital to army operations, **Wing Commander Hugh Malcolm** led his Blenheim squadron, without a fighter escort, on a successful attack in North Africa. He took on the hugely difficult mission in support of essential ground troop operations, even though he was aware that the lack of fighter cover would be fraught with extreme danger. So it proved, and while his flight successfully carried out their mission they were intercepted by the enemy during their return and shot down one by one.

Flight Sergeant Arthur Aaron was fatally injured by a fighter attack on his Stirling aircraft in November 1943, on a raid to Turin. He suffered appalling bullet wounds to his face, shattering his jaw, he was struck in the lung and his right arm was rendered useless. Displaying remarkable courage and fortitude, he nevertheless managed to direct his surviving crew to a safe landing. He died nine hours later.

In November 1943, badly wounded in the head, shoulders and hands, **Flight Lieutenant William Reid** was on the way to bomb a target in Dusseldorf. Despite his injuries, and despite casualties amongst his crew, Flight Lieutenant Reid pressed on, bombed accurately, and got his aircraft home.

Despite repeated fighter attacks which damaged his Halifax aircraft, **Pilot Officer Cyril Barton** pressed on with a raid on Nuremberg. Misreading a signal, some of

his crew had evacuated the plane. He was left unable to communicate with the rest of the crew, but nonetheless single-handedly bombed the target, then brought his wounded crewmen home. His aircraft was so damaged that a crash landing had to be undertaken, which cost the young pilot his life.

After completing 110 missions, **Squadron Leader Robert Palmer** led a formation of Lancasters to Cologne in December 1943. With two engines ablaze he marked the target perfectly for the following bombers – then spiralled down in flames.

Twice attacked by a fighter and with two engines out, as a "master bomber", **Captain Edwin Swales** remained over the target at Pforzheim in 1945, giving instructions to other bombers. Over friendly territory, he held his Lancaster steady while his crew baled out – then was killed as the aircraft crashed.

Struggling to control his burning Lancaster, **Squadron Leader Ian Bazalgette** accurately marked the target for the main force then died trying to save his wounded crew.

Leading eleven Ventura aircraft on a daylight raid in May 1943, **Squadron Leader Leonard Trent** bombed an Amsterdam power station in a display of outstanding leadership, despite intense fighter attack from 15 – 20 planes, resulting in the loss of every bomber. He was taken prisoner after being forced to bale out of his aircraft.

Squadron Leader Arthur Scarf was the pilot of a lone surviving Blenheim bomber in 1941 when he attacked a Japanese fighter base in Thailand, meeting fierce fighter opposition and ground fire that led to him being mortally wounded. Despite his wounds, he managed to crash land in safe territory which ensured his crew survived.

Pilot Officer Arthur Mynarski was the mid upper gunner on his Lancaster bomber on a raid over France when it was attacked by a fighter and set ablaze. The order was given to abandon the aircraft and he was badly burned in a desperate and unsuccessful effort to rescue the trapped rear gunner. He was eventually forced to bale out, his clothes and parachute on fire, and died from his injuries. Miraculously, the rear gunner survived the crash and testified that his colleague's efforts to save him had undoubtedly cost the Pilot Officer his own life.

Leonard Cheshire and **Guy Gibson** also received the Victoria Cross – their stories are covered in Chapter Four. Many other acts of extraordinary heroism must surely have gone unreported, with no witnesses left to testify to courage displayed. Yet these stories remind us of the sacrifice made by so many.

CHAPTER 4
The Dambusters

The night of May 16ᵗʰ, 1943, was clear and moonlit as 19 specially modified planes took off on what was to become one of the most famous episodes of the Second World War.

The planes were Lancasters and they took off in three waves from their base at RAF Scampton in Lincolnshire, on a mission so secret the aircrews had only been briefed the night before, and testing completed the previous day.

This was 617 Squadron – The Dambusters. Of the 19 planes that left Lincolnshire that night only eleven returned. In human terms, 53 of the 133 men taking part lost their lives, and a further two were captured.

But despite the heavy losses, the extraordinary achievements – both human and technical – made the raid on the Ruhr dams one of the most celebrated moments of the entire conflict.

A desire to damage Germany's industrial might, so destroying its ability to support its own war effort, had long been a key

Barnes Wallis

plank in the British Government's strategy. Prime Minister Winston Churchill believed the RAF, and Bomber Command in particular, had a key role to play in taking the war to the heartland of Germany.

In February of 1943, Vickers Armstrong scientist, Barnes Wallis, revealed his idea for a "bouncing bomb" designed to attack dams. If successful, it would deprive German heavy industry of its vital supplies of water. The bomb, codenamed "Upkeep", was designed to maximise the chances of actually hitting a dam, a difficult task in the days before computer guided weaponry systems. In order to be successful, the bomb had to be dropped from 60 feet, at an angle of seven degrees from the horizontal, at a ground speed of 220mph, between 425 and 475 yards from the target and with back spin. If all of this was achieved, the bomb would bounce across the surface of the water, strike the dam wall, sink underwater and explode.

Barnes Wallis was ordered to work fast, to prepare his bombs for an attack on the Mohne, Eder and Sorpe dams in the Ruhr, planned for May of that year.

The Bouncing Bomb

Reculver Bay Reconnaissance

Guy Gibson in Flying Gear

Mohne Dam Breached

The idea first came to Wallis early in 1942, as he began experimenting skipping marbles over water tanks in his garden. In turn, this led to his writing a paper in April 1942 entitled "Spherical Bomb — Surface Torpedo".

He believed a bomb could skip over the surface of water, avoiding torpedo nets, and sink directly next to a dam wall, with the water concentrating the force of the explosion on the target.

The addition of backspin was a crucial piece in the jigsaw. This was needed to make the bomb skip along behind the dropping aircraft reducing the chance of the aircraft being blown up or brought down by the force of the explosion below. It also prevented the bomb from moving away from the target wall as it sank.

Air Chief Marshal Sir Arthur "Bomber" Harris, Commander of Bomber Command, was ordered to form a special squadron to deliver the mission, and 617 Squadron was formed. An exceptional officer had to be found to command the mission, and Harris personally selected 24-year-old Wing Commander, Guy Gibson.

Gibson was already a highly decorated flier, having been awarded the Distinguished Service Order and the Distinguished Flying Cross and Bar. The operation was codenamed "Chastise". Even Gibson was not told its purpose for several weeks.

Intensive testing took place at Reculver Bay in Kent, and the tests were only completed the day before the raid took place.

The raid began after midnight on May 17th. Gibson himself led the first wave in its attack on the Mohne Dam. His bomb was released at 28 minutes past midnight but despite hitting the target and detonating, it failed to breach the dam. The second and third aircraft were forced to abort their attacks under intense anti-aircraft fire. The next bomber in was flown by Squadron Leader Henry Melvin Young, but Gibson accompanied him on his approach, seeking to divert fire to his own aircraft to help Young. The strategy worked and the dam finally breached. Gibson continued to circle low, seeking to attract enemy fire away from his colleagues as they attacked.

Soon after, a second wave of Lancasters, led by Gibson, flew to the Eder Dam. Again, the first two bombs failed to breach its wall, but shortly before 2am it was destroyed by the bomber flown by Pilot Officer Les Knight.

Guy Gibson

By now heavy mist had gathered, making the mission almost impossible for the third wave of five bombers to locate their target. The dam was damaged, but not breached, and two of the aircraft were shot down.

Reconnaissance photographs were taken within hours. These showed the damaged dams and the resulting dramatic destruction brought about by flooding. The news was

Eder Dam 1943

53

greeted with joy by all at home: the King, the Prime Minister and ordinary people were all unanimous in their praise of the mission.

The Germans repaired the dams quickly, but they could not repair the very significant flooding damage done to the Ruhr. In total, eleven factories were destroyed, 114 seriously damaged, 25 road and rail bridges were swept away, and throughout the entire region power and water supplies were disrupted. Roads and canals were affected, and more than 50 hectares of agricultural land was flooded. The flooding caused more than 1,300 casualties.

For the remainder of the war, 10,000 German troops were diverted from front line conflict in order to guard the dams.

For his own outstanding leadership and bravery, Guy Gibson was awarded the Victoria Cross. A further 32 members of the squadron also received gallantry awards for their parts in the raid.

Gibson joined the RAF in 1936, and even before the Dambuster raid had built a formidable reputation as a tough and talented officer.

After the raid, he was feted as a national hero and was the most highly decorated officer in the RAF. As such, his commanders saw that his loss or capture would be a serious blow to morale, and a boost to the Germans, and against his own wishes he was confined to non-operational duties.

This included a lecture tour of the United States. At that time, American airmen were being sent home exhausted, pronounced "tour expired" after flying 25 operations. During one question time Gibson was asked how many operations he had flown over Germany. He answered "174" to a stunned silence.

He was not to be sidelined for long. He pestered Bomber Command to return to operational duties, and eventually his wish was granted. In September 1944, he appointed himself as the master bomber on a night-time raid over Germany. His task was to help control the raid, guiding the bombers to their target.

Tragically, he did not return in his Mosquito. After orchestrating the attack, his plane was seen plunging into the ground at Steenbergen in Holland. Mystery continues to surround the cause of the crash.

Lancaster Bomber

Barnes Wallis described him as a man of "great courage and adventure" for whom inactivity was a slow death. "He had seen countless friends and comrades perish in the great crusade. Perhaps something in him even welcomed the inevitability he had always felt, that before the war ended he would join them in their Bomber Command Valhalla. He had pushed his luck beyond all limits and he knew it. But that was the kind of man he was ... a man of great courage, inspiration and leadership. A man born for war ... but born to fall in war."

He was 26 years old.

Guy Gibson

CHAPTER 5
The Battle of Britain

On June 18th, 1940, following the routing of the Allied forces in France and the evacuation from Dunkirk, Britain held its breath and waited for a German invasion.

Speaking on the BBC, Prime Minister Winston Churchill told the nation:

The Battle of France is over. I expect that the Battle of Britain is about to begin. Upon this battle depends the survival of Christian civilisation. Upon it depends our own British life, and the long continuity of our institutions and our Empire. The whole fury and might of the enemy must very soon be turned on us.

Hitler knows that he will have to break us in this Island or lose the war. If we can stand up to him, all Europe may be free and the life of the world may move forward into broad, sunlit uplands. But if we fail, then the whole world, including the United States, including all that we have known and cared for, will sink into the abyss of a new Dark Age made more sinister, and perhaps more protracted, by the lights of a perverted science.

Let us therefore brace ourselves to our duties, and so bear ourselves that – if the British Empire and its Commonwealth last for a thousand years – men will still say "This was their finest hour."

The battle for Britain had begun. Germany stood poised across the Channel, ready to invade. Operation Sealion saw the Germans assemble hundreds of invasion barges along the French and Dutch coastal ports. The intention was to land 160,000 men along a 44-mile stretch of the south-eastern coast of Britain. Around 3,000 Luftwaffe planes were positioned within striking distance.

While the pilots of Fighter Command resisted the attempts of the Luftwaffe to gain aerial dominance over the skies of Britain, Bomber Command was tasked with carrying out repeated attacks on the fleet of 2,000 invasion barges along with fuel supplies and air bases. Hitler was concerned at the ability of the RAF to be a significant threat to his plan.

Hermann Goering, head of the Luftwaffe, was instructed by Hitler that the RAF must be "beaten down to such an extent that it can no longer muster any power of attack worth mentioning against the German crossing."

On paper, the Luftwaffe had an advantage in terms of the number of planes and

Robert Watson-Watt

Bawdsey led to the creation of a chain of radar stations throughout the east and south coast of England. This was to prove a vital part of British defences during the Battle of Britain.

The system meant that Fighter Command was given an early warning of an incoming attack by the Luftwaffe and could react accordingly. In 1940, Watson-Watt and his team further improved their system, which allowed Fighter Command to detect incoming enemy planes from a much greater distance, giving more time to get organised to repel an attack.

Throughout the years, much attention has rightly been given to the young pilots who stood up to the might of the Luftwaffe over the skies of Britain from the middle of July 1943.

Initially, the German air force attacked shipping in the English Channel and the nation's coastal defences. Then the focus moved to the destruction of the RAF.

Goering sent his forces to attack airfields and radar bases. He sought to engage British fighter

pilots, in particular, pilots with experience. However, the RAF also held a few aces. The German planes had fairly short operational range and so had limited time to reach Britain and carry out their missions. In addition, of course, they had to fly over enemy territory.

The RAF had one other major advantage – radar.

One of the unsung heroes of the Battle of Britain is Robert Watson-Watt, the man credited with inventing radar. He had developed a fascination with radio waves and what they could do. In particular, he became intrigued with the idea of using radio waves to detect aircraft. In February 1935 he took part in a successful trial in which short wave radio was used to detect a bomber.

He was then appointed Superintendent of the Air Ministry's Bawdsey Research Station near Felixstowe in Suffolk. The work at

planes and pilots with his own fighters, believing that since Germany had more machines and more experienced pilots, the engagement would break Fighter Command.

Within a month, in September, the Germans were frustrated that British fighters were still able to engage with them in significant numbers, and on Hitler's orders a campaign of bombing against major cities began. Then, in mid-September, the Nazis launched a colossal aerial offensive on what is now known as "Battle of Britain Day." The German forces were savaged by the RAF in the skies over southern Britain and two days later, on September 17th, Hitler postponed his plan to invade Britain.

The Battle of Britain had been won.

The average age of an RAF pilot in 1940 was 20, with some as young as 18. In those days many of the RAF's Battle of Britain pilots were not old enough to vote (21 was the age of majority at that time). However, they were old enough to risk their lives in the face of a desperate battle to save Britain from the Nazis.

Fighter Command had an international and cosmopolitan make-up. Fighting alongside the British were many nationalities. There were Poles (141), Czechs (87), Belgians (24) and Free French (13) swelling the ranks.

Of the RAF pilots who flew in the Battle of Britain, around two-thirds were officers earning around £264 per annum,

equivalent to a little more than £30,000 today. The other third were made up of sergeant and flight sergeant pilots who, despite sharing the risk, earned considerably less.

Many aircrew played a vital role in the weeks of intensive aerial combat over Britain during the two months. However, it is right that one or two of them are worthy of particular mention.

The man charged with leading Fighter Command, and so keeping the German Air Force at bay, was Air Chief Marshall Sir Hugh Dowding. The Scot had been due to retire in 1939, but was asked to stay on as the war loomed and then hostilities broke out. He was nicknamed "Stuffy," and had lived up

to his name in the early months of the war by resisting repeated requests from Churchill to weaken the home defences by sending more squadrons to the war in France.

It is Dowding who is largely credited with developing the integrated air defence system, and for superb marshalling of the resources at his disposal which thwarted Goering's attempts to destroy Fighter Command. The inscription on his statue – which stands on the Strand in London – says:

With remarkable foresight he ensured the equipment of his command with monoplane fighters, the Spitfire and the Hurricane. He was among the first to appreciate the vital importance of radar and an

effective command and control system for his squadrons. They were ready when war came. In the preliminary stages of that war, he thoroughly trained his minimal forces and conserved them against strong political pressure to disperse and misuse them. His wise and prudent judgement and leadership helped to ensure victory against overwhelming odds and prevented the loss of the Battle of Britain and probably the whole war.

To him, the people of Britain and of the Free World owe largely the life and liberties they enjoy today.

Dowding retired in October 1940, immediately after the Battle of Britain.

Hugh Dowding

near Southampton in August 1940. He was injured in one eye and one foot, his engine was damaged and his fuel tank set on fire.

As he struggled to free himself from his plane, he saw another German fighter. He managed to get back into his seat and fired on the enemy plane until it was destroyed. He baled out and parachuted to safety, only to be fired upon by members of the Home Guard.

Nicolson was awarded the Victoria Cross for his deed – the only Battle of Britain pilot to be so honoured.

Eric Nicolson

Wing Commander Eric Nicolson was just 23 years old, and a Flight Lieutenant, when his Hurricane was fired on by a German fighter

He was killed when an RAF B-24 in which he was flying caught fire and crashed into the Bay of Bengal.

The London Gazette of November 15th, 1940, said:

The London Gazette
𝔓𝔲𝔟𝔩𝔦𝔰𝔥𝔢𝔡 𝔟𝔶 𝔄𝔲𝔱𝔥𝔬𝔯𝔦𝔱𝔶

During an engagement with the enemy near Southampton Flt Lt Nicolson's aircraft was hit by four cannon shells, two of which wounded him whilst another set fire to the gravity tank. When about to abandon his aircraft owing to flames in the cockpit he sighted an enemy fighter. This he attacked and shot down. Although as a result of staying in his burning aircraft he sustained serious burns to his hands, face, neck and legs.

Despite his injuries, Nicolson was fully recovered by the end of 1941 and returned to operational duties in 1942 when he was posted to India as a Squadron Leader. During this time he was also awarded the Distinguished Flying Cross and promoted to Wing Commander.

In his famous speech of August 20th, 1940, Churchill paid wonderful tribute to the airmen of Fighter Command.

The gratitude of every home in our Island, in our Empire, and indeed throughout the world, except in the abodes of the guilty, goes out to the British airmen who, undaunted by odds, unwearied in their constant challenge and mortal danger, are turning the tide of the world war by their prowess and by their devotion. Never in the field of human conflict was so much owed by so many to so few.

In all, just under 3,000 British pilots took part in the Battle of Britain. Of this number, 544 lost their lives, with many others suffering injuries.

THE PLANES

Two planes were to become synonymous with fighting off the German Air Force – the Hurricane and the Spitfire. This partnership dominated the defence of Britain in the skies. Both aircraft were single-seat monoplanes carrying four pairs of Browning machine guns, and they were only a few months apart in terms of entering service.

The Hurricane

The Supermarine Spitfire had an advanced wing design, used lightweight alloys and a more powerful engine. The result was a leap forward in the development of monoplane aircraft design and engine technology which was shared by both aircraft.

The Spitfire was one of the most important military aircraft of all time, and the Mk1 version entered service in August 1938, bringing a superior performance and hard-hitting firepower that made it a formidable opponent in aerial combat.

The Hawker designed and built Hurricane was much more robust than either the Spitfire or its German adversaries, and was able to absorb a huge amount of battle damage that would have downed other planes. It outnumbered the Spitfire roughly two to one during the Battle and is credited with shooting down 656 enemy fighters and bombers against 529 for Spitfires.

The first Hurricanes entered service in December 1937 and by August 1940, when Goering threw everything he had at the RAF, its airfields and radar stations, 28 of the 55 fighter squadrons were equipped with the Hurricane.

The Spitfire

CHAPTER 6
Two Special Legacies

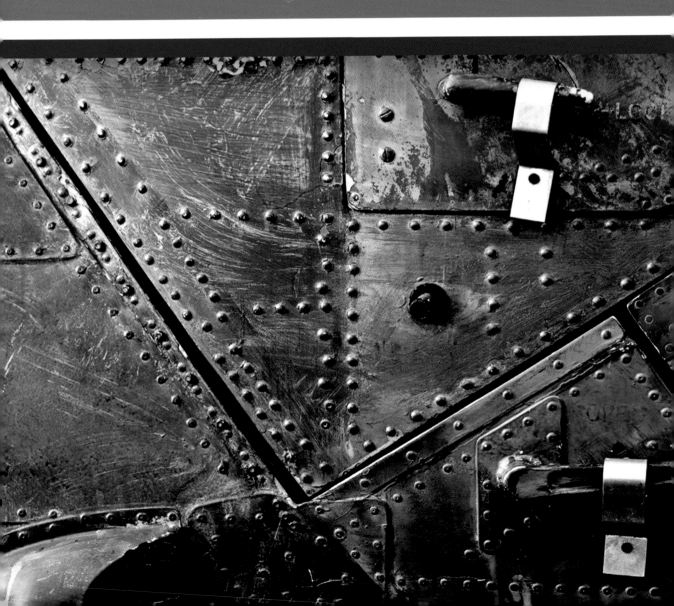

Two of the RAF's greatest heroes are nowadays remembered as much for the huge contribution they made to wider society after the war as they are for the outstanding courage they showed during the fighting.

Leonard Cheshire and Douglas Bader – two men whose skill and courage as pilots made them legendary – both went on to establish charitable organisations dedicated to helping others.

Group Captain Leonard Cheshire was a much decorated bomber pilot. He was awarded the Distinguished Service Order for flying a badly damaged bomber back to base in November 1940, and was given a job as commander of the legendary 617 "Dambusters" Squadron in September 1943.

Cheshire was the only airman to win the Victoria Cross for an extended period of sustained courage and outstanding effort, rather than a single act of valour.

The London Gazette of September 8th 1944 reported his lengthy and distinguished service in the RAF. This included the fact that he had volunteered to relinquish the rank of Group Captain in order to be returned to operational duties. He also pioneered a new form of target marking over Munich:

Leonard Cheshire

The London Gazette
Published by Authority

Wing Commander Cheshire has now completed a total of 100 missions. In four years of fighting against the bitterest opposition he has maintained a record of outstanding personal achievement, placing himself invariably in the forefront of the battle. What he did in the Munich operation was typical of the careful planning, brilliant execution and contempt for danger which has established for Wing Commander Cheshire a reputation second to none in Bomber Command.

In 1948, Cheshire founded the charity now styled Leonard Cheshire Disability, with a residential home for disabled ex-servicemen at Le Court. The charity now provides support to disabled people in almost 50 countries throughout the world. It is currently one of the top 30 British charities. With his wife, Sue Ryder, he went on to set up a number of other charitable organizations, notably The Ryder-Cheshire Foundation, begun at the time of their marriage in 1959. It now mainly operates in two fields: the rehabilitation of disabled people, through Ryder-Cheshire Volunteers, and the prevention and treatment of tuberculosis, through Target Tuberculosis. Cheshire was made a life peer in 1991.

Leonard Cheshire died of motor neurone disease in 1992, aged 74.

Douglas Bader

of Britain. He was awarded the Distinguished Flying Cross with Bar, and the Distinguished Service Order with Bar.

In August 1941 he was brought down over France. He described how he baled out.

The ground below was the farm and grazing land of northern France. A man wearing a peaked sort of railway porter's cap and a blue smock, carrying on his shoulders a yoke to which were attached two buckets, was opening a gate between two grass fields. A woman with a scarf was with him. As he opened the gate, he noticed me about 800 feet above and in front of him. They both remained motionless, staring. I then realized my appearance was a bit odd. My right leg was no longer with me. It had caught somewhere in the top of the cockpit as I tried to leave my Spitfire.

Douglas Bader was, and remains, the most famous fighter ace of World War Two.

The 1950s film "Reach for The Sky", based on the book of the same name, told the story of his life, and starred the movie idol Kenneth More as Bader.

His was a truly inspirational story. After joining the RAF in 1928, Bader – a fearless aerobatic flyer – crashed attempting a slow roll. He lost both legs and was retired on medical grounds. His career in the RAF was, for the time being, over.

He was determined to recover and fly again, however, and remarkably managed to rehabilitate himself. At the outbreak of World War Two he persuaded the RAF to let him fly again, this time with artificial legs, and passed all of his flight checks.

A brilliant fighter leader, he was given command of 242 Squadron and led them throughout the Battle

Colditz

his former colleagues from Fighter Command – formed the Douglas Bader Foundation in his honour. The mission of the foundation at its inception was to continue his work in conjunction with and on behalf of individuals with a disability.

The first initiative came to fruition in 1993 with the completion of the Douglas Bader Centre, a facility built at Queen Mary's Hospital, Roehampton, in West London to support rehabilitation services for amputees. Now called The Douglas Bader Rehabilitation Centre, it provides a range of facilities and services for people who have gone through an amputation, including a Walking School and Rehabilitation Therapy Groups.

He saw out the remainder of the war as a prisoner – despite many escape attempts – eventually ending up in the infamous Colditz prison.

After the war Bader considered politics for a while but, instead, chose to join the giant Shell corporation. The decision was based on his desire to repay a debt. Shell had been ready to take him on, aged 23, after his accident. So although other companies were now offering him more money, he went with Shell, eventually taking control of their aircraft group which employed around 250,000 people, and becoming chairman of Shell Aircraft Ltd. He was internationally famous as a sought-after speaker on aviation, and spent much time travelling the world.

The Queen Mary's Hospital had provided Sir Douglas's medical care as an amputee for 50 years.

Bader was a tireless campaigner on disability issues throughout his adult life, and was knighted for his efforts in 1976. He died in 1982 from a sudden heart attack. The same year Bader's family and friends – including many of

CHAPTER 7
After the World Wars

The men and women of the RAF have continued to serve their country around the world since the end of the Second World War. Wherever British forces have been needed, the nation's airmen and women have served.

In particular, the RAF has played important roles in some of the major post-war conflicts, including the Falklands, the Gulf War and Iraq, and continues to serve with great distinction in Afghanistan. They have also served in Malaya, in Kosovo, Kenya, even in Korea.

Since the end of the Second World War, technological advances have accelerated,

with supersonic jet aircraft and high technology weapons systems now in use. Nonetheless, the human requirements remain constant – absolute professionalism, courage, compassion and devotion to duty remain hallmarks of the RAF.

In this final section we look at how the RAF has played a pivotal role in a number of conflicts over the past few decades, and at some of the brave men and women who have gone "Through Adversity to the Stars."

FALKLANDS WAR

Although its role has often been overshadowed by the more visible presence of both the Royal Navy and the Army, the RAF played an important role in the conflict to reclaim the Falkland Islands in the South Atlantic after they were invaded by Argentine forces in 1982.

RAF Harrier jet pilots, and RAF helicopter pilots joined their Royal Navy pilot colleagues in flying many dangerous missions in hostile territory and against a dangerous foe.

The first RAF aircraft to operate from an aircraft carrier, HMS Hermes, was the RAF's Number One (Fighter) Squadron of Harriers, led by then Wing Commander Peter Squire. His squadron of six jets flew more than 150 sorties, with pilots often flying twice a day. Dangerous low level flights were made in order to launch ground attacks on enemy forces.

Three of the Harriers were brought down by enemy fire, and one was forced to crash land. Wing Commander Squire became the first RAF officer to launch a laser-guided smart bomb, attacking Argentine troops on Mount Longdon. Sir Peter Squire's awards include the Distinguished Flying Cross and the Air Force Cross. He went on to become Chief of Air Staff.

He was not alone in being recognised for his bravery and devotion to duty. The London Gazette of October 8th, 1982, records awards made to several others, including Squadron Leader Robert Tuxford and Flight Lieutenant Alan Swan.

The London Gazette

Squadron Leader Tuxford was awarded the Air Force Cross for his role in a daring refuelling operation essential to support the first Vulcan bombing raid on Port Stanley airfield, the famous Black Buck operations.

He was captain of a Victor K2 Tanker supporting the raid on April 30th, 1982, and his task was to pass on fuel to another tanker which, in turn, would refuel a Vulcan en route to the target. This relay was essential to ensure the bombers had sufficient fuel for the extreme, long-range missions from RAF Ascension Island.

The London Gazette reported:

... during the refueling manoeuvre, the Victor flew into violent thunderstorms and suffered turbulence so severe that the receiving probe was broken from the Victor aircraft. Immediately, the aircraft reversed roles and Squadron Leader Tuxford took on the fuel load. However, the delay resulted in the fuel transfer being completed further from Ascension Island than planned and Squadron Leader Tuxford's aircraft did not receive all the fuel required to complete the mission. Nevertheless, in the full knowledge that his aircraft would run out of fuel some 400 nautical miles south of Ascension Island on its return and in spite of the obvious risk, Squadron Leader Tuxford transferred the full amount required by the Vulcan to complete its bombing mission. Moreover, at that time he was not able to seek assistance from Ascension Island, because to have broken radio silence would have jeopardized the safety of the Vulcan en route to its target. His determination and courage were rewarded however, when, after the Vulcan cleared the target area, a reserve tanker was successfully scrambled from Ascension Island and Squadron Leader Tuxford's aircraft made a safe recovery. Squadron Leader Tuxford's selfless devotion to duty ensured the success of the Vulcan mission and was in the finest traditions of the Royal Air Force.

Patrolling the Falklands

Tornados patrolling skies over Falklands

On other occasions he had to remove napalm, and once, a 1,000 pound unexploded Argentinian bomb, of the same type that had previously killed an army bomb disposal expert. The bomb was too close to the headquarters to be dealt with by demolition.

The London Gazette said:

Flight Lieutenant Alan Swan was awarded the Queen's Gallantry Medal for his coolness and courage in tackling dangerous unexploded ordnance throughout the campaign, in particular an unexploded bomb which threatened the safety of wounded service men and women being treated at a hospital at Ajax Bay.

Flight Lieutenant Swan was commanding a bomb disposal unit from the RAF Armament Support Unit when, on May 27th, following an air attack, two unexploded bombs were found next to the operating theatre at the Command Logistics Hospital and the ground outside was scattered with explosives.

The London Gazette

Regardless of the imminent danger to his own life, Flight Lieutenant Swan defused the bomb and the headquarters continued in operation without interruption. Throughout the campaign, Flight Lieutenant Swan displayed qualities of leadership, courage and coolness which were a magnificent example to others.

Defence Harrier

When Iraq invaded Kuwait on August 2nd, 1990, the international outcry was overwhelming in its condemnation for the actions of the regime of Saddam Hussein.

Within 48 hours the international response was underway, and twelve RAF Tornado F3 interceptors had arrived in Saudi Arabia alongside aircraft from the US Air Force. They were soon joined by Jaguar and further Tornado aircraft from the UK and redeployed from Germany.

Nimrod maritime patrol aircraft followed, with VC10 tanker aircraft. The build-up continued, and by mid-January 1991 RAF strength stood at 18 Tornado F3 fighters, 46 Tornado strike and reconnaissance aircraft, 17 tankers, three Nimrods, twelve Chinook helicopters, 19 Pumas and seven Hercules aircraft. Buccaneers were also soon to join. Eventually, some 7,000 RAF personnel were directly involved.

In all, the RAF took part in more than 6,000 sorties – more than any other nation except the USA.

Wing Commander John Broadbent was awarded the Distinguished Service Order, announced in the London Gazette in June 1991, for his role in the conflict. In particular, he was praised for his work in creating an effective Tornado fighting force, and for his role in flying 21 operational missions himself, including some of the most dangerous of the campaign.

Tornado

The London Gazette

Wing Commander John Broadbent
His outstanding gallantry and fortitude in the face of the enemy, and his superb leadership and example are in the highest traditions of the Royal Air Force.

ZA718

As Saddam Hussein's regime was viewed as an increased threat, the USA and UK mounted plans to invade Iraq in 2003, concerned that the dictator was developing weapons of mass destruction. American and British forces were to remain in the gulf state for years.

At the same time, Squadron Leader William Browne, a Buccaneer navigator, was awarded the Distinguished Flying Cross. Described as *"the most outstanding navigator of the Buccaneer detachment"* he led the first combined Buccaneer/Tornado attacks against heavily defended enemy positions deep in Iraqi territory:

Again, a large deployment of RAF aircraft and personnel was mobilized, including strike aircraft and a combination of attack and other helicopters.

This conflict was also to see a significant development in the history of British gallantry awards, when Flight Lieutenant Michelle Goodman became the first woman to be awarded the Distinguished Flying

The London Gazette

Squadron Leader William Browne
By rising instantly to the demands made of him, and through the exceptional results he achieved in confronting the enemy in the heart of his territory, he has shown himself to be a magnificent leader under fire.

Merlin delivering to Iraq

Flight Lieutenant Michelle Goodman

Cross for her actions on June 1st, 2007. A helicopter pilot, she was called out that night to help rescue a casualty in an isolated British location in the centre of Basra, where a mortar attack had taken place. She was warned that landing a helicopter at the location was viewed as high risk, with the helicopter a potential target.

She had to fly at a low level across the hostile areas of the city, using night vision goggles, in the face of intense enemy fire, and then had to execute a dangerous landing at an unfamiliar site. When the casualty was loaded, she took off, launching flares as a counter measure against detected incoming missiles.

Her citation read:

Without the Instant Reaction Team intervention, the casualty would have died within 15 minutes. Despite extreme pressure, whilst in the face of the enemy, she made the right decision. This was a bold and daring sortie which undoubtedly saved life.

Her own description provides an insight.

On our approach we could see several flashes around us but chose to continue. At about 20 feet the dust was so bad that I could not see the ground, I was now relying on Sergeant Steve Thomas to guide me safely to the ground. The time it would have cost to go around and re-do the approach was unacceptable to the casualty.

Chinook

On the ground the rockets were getting closer but the medics are highly proficient at what they do, so within five minutes we were getting airborne again. As the helicopter rose above the rooftops four rocket propelled grenades were fired in our direction. Fifteen minutes after the call out we were landing at the hospital so the soldier could get the medical care that was vital for his survival.

Wherever the RAF is stationed, it is the task of the RAF Regiment and the RAF Police to ensure the safety of bases. The courage shown by Corporal David Hayden of the RAF Regiment in Iraq earned him a Military Cross.

Whilst deployed to Basra in 2007, he dashed across open ground to save a wounded comrade, even though he came under fire from a force of around 50 insurgent gunmen. Corporal Hayden managed to reach Leading Aircraftsman Martin Beard, who had been grievously wounded, and carried him more than 200 metres. nfortunately, although Corporal Hayden had no way of knowing, the casualty had already died from his wounds.

When presented with his medal – one of the highest awards for gallantry – by The Queen in 2008 he modestly insisted he was "no hero." It was the first time the Military Cross had been awarded to an RAF airman. He said: "If anyone's a hero it's the lads that have passed away and their families – they're heroes. They are dealing with a lot more than what I am dealing with."

Leading Aircraftsman Beard's family disagreed. His sister Victoria told the media: "It was extremely dangerous, and the obstacles and danger he faced were unbelievable… It was entirely thanks to David that we were able to fly Martin home, and I can't thank him enough."

Corporal Hayden's citation quoted his *"outstanding gallantry, selflessness and personal example in the face of a particularly ferocious attack from a determined enemy."*

AFGHANISTAN

The invasion of Afghanistan in 2001 followed the terrorist strike against the World Trade Centre. Afghanistan was seen as a training ground for global terror organizations, in particular Al Qaeda, and political leaders took the decision to invade to reduce the threat posed.

The USA and UK again acted in concert, with the RAF providing the use of bases, air-to-air re-fuelling tankers and reconnaissance aircraft. RAF Harriers were later involved, as were Tornados. A significant helicopter force has also been involved throughout the period.

The helicopters have played a particular role in flying ground troops around the mountainous and rugged terrain, and in recovering casualties. Throughout the years of RAF involvement in Afghanistan there have been some outstanding examples of skill and daring.

Flight Lieutenant Dan Cullen was awarded the Distinguished Flying Cross for his role in averting a catastrophic loss of life.

He saved the lives of 30 men as he flew one-handed, 50 feet above the ground, in order to prevent his co-pilot, who had been shot by the Taliban, falling onto his controls. The aircraft was travelling at more than 100 knots at the time and a crash would almost certainly have killed all on board.

Tornado

Tornado taking off from Kandahar

Flight Lieutenant Cullen and his crew flew the lead Chinook helicopter in a formation of two aircraft sent to pick up 60 men. The ground troops had been clearing a Taliban improvised explosive device (IED) factory in Helmand Province in April 2011. As the men sprinted to board the aircraft, insurgent gunners opened fire and a bullet smashed through Dan's cockpit window, missing him by inches and hitting his co-pilot in the leg.

Cullen, of 18(B) Squadron, based at RAF Oldham, Hants, said: "The next 30 seconds were the longest of my life as I fought every natural instinct to take off."

His co-pilot managed to stay conscious long enough to assist with the take-off, then went into shock, lost consciousness and slumped onto the controls. As a result the aircraft's nose dipped and it headed for an impact with the ground. Dan had to restrain the slumped colleague with one hand, while flying with the other, and at the same time handling all navigation and communications until crewmen in the back managed to revive the pilot and pull him from the cockpit.

The citation for Dan, who had served five tours of duty in Afghanistan at the time, states:

Throughout this incident Cullen maintained a sublime level of composure that was an inspiration to his crew. His personal courage, strong leadership, exceptional flying skills and rapid intervention were directly responsible for the safe recovery of the troops and his aircraft.

Merlin

Flight Lieutenant Dan Cullen

Although Flight Lieutenant Cullen told his father of the rescue, his mother only discovered the extent of the danger her son had faced when the Ministry of Defence released the honours list. His explanation? "I didn't want to worry my mother."

Tornado

Another Chinook pilot was also recognised for his service in 2011, when Flight Lieutenant Michael Anderson was awarded the Distinguished Flying Cross after rescuing Afghan children caught in a firefight.

Flight Lieutenant Anderson had to land under heavy Taliban mortar fire to rescue the six injured children in Helmand province.

His citation read:

Anderson's courage, and his calm, highly professional display of captaincy enabled the entire crew to conduct a textbook helicopter medical evacuation in the face of a bold, determined and coordinated enemy.

The pilot was the captain of an Immediate Response Team – a Chinook unit at Camp Bastion in Helmand Province that is constantly on stand-by to collect injured personnel and civilians from the battlefield. He was flying to the scene of an explosion, flanked by two American Pave Hawk helicopters and an Apache helicopter, when he received reports of mortar and heavy machine-gun fire at the landing site.

While the two American aircraft fired back at Taliban fighters, the Chinook landed, picked up the injured children, and flew back to Camp Bastion.

Chinook

Flight Lieutenant Alexander "Frenchie" Duncan was honoured with the Air Force Cross at the same time. He already had a DFC, which he won two years previously, flying a Chinook hit by a rocket-propelled grenade. His Air Force Cross was for rescuing a soldier injured by an improvised explosive device. He had already picked up one casualty when he received a report of another at a Forward Operating Base in Helmand Province, where conflict with the Taliban is rife.

The citation read:

Time and fuel were running low, and despite the knowledge that the landing site was under fire, Duncan committed the aircraft and executed a textbook approach and landed in no more than 200m visibility and with zero illumination, safely picking up the casualty who was then safely recovered back to Camp Bastion hospital.

Since the Royal Flying Corps was first established 100 years ago, Britain has been safer and better protected thanks to the unstinting efforts of its airmen and women.

Whether flying in the skies over Britain, whether policing our interests around the world, pilots, navigators, gunners, and ground crew, all have played a vital role in defending those freedoms which we all hold dear, but never more so than at times of crisis and conflict.

THE ROYAL AIR FORCE SQUADRONAIRES

NEW ALBUM OUT AUTUMN 2012

O ROYAL AIR FORCE

SQUADRONAIRES
AND TODD GORDON

HELPING *the* HEROES

With reinforcements:
Clare Teal, Jacqui Dankworth, Horse, The Swingcats, Carol Kidd and Eddi Reader

IN SUPPORT OF
HELP *for* HEROES

(I've Got a Gal in) Kalamazoo • I Left My Heart in San Francisco • Who Wants to be a Millionaire? • Autumn in New York
I Believe in You • My Favorite Things • They Can't Take That Away from Me • Summer Wind • Come Back to Me • Cheek to Cheek
Evergreen • Let's Do It • Manhattan • The Best Is Yet to Come

FOR MORE DETAILS. VISIT WWW.TODDGORDON.COM

Acknowledgements and Credits:

Contains public sector information licensed under the Open Government Licence v1.0.

Our thanks to The London Gazette and The National Archives for information about awarding medals to individuals for gallantry.

Pictures

Cover	Poster © Image: IWM (Art PST.14810) Every effort has been made to trace copyright.
Cover	LA(phot) Billy Bunting /© UK MOD Crown Copyright 2012
Cover	Harland Quarrington /© UK MOD Crown Copyright 2007
Cover	SAC Neil Chapman /© UK MOD Crown Copyright 2010
Cover, 36	© Matt Gibson, Shutterstock, 83921362
Cover, 38	Poster © Image: IWM (Art PST.14222) Every effort has been made to trace copyright.
Cover	Sgt Pete Mobbs/©MOD Crown Copyright (2008)
Cover	©Carole Castelli, Shutterstock, 14861653
2-3	© David Fowler/Shutterstock.com, 68596804
4-5	© Piotr Zajc/Shutterstock.com, 72737485
6-7	© Kenneth William Caleno, Shutterstock, 5190115
8, etc	© Sean Gladwell, Shutterstock, 24903724
9	© T. Gagnon, Image: Library of Congress, Photographic Prints 1910-1920, LC-USZ62-89969
9	© Keith Gentry/Shutterstock.com, 35785333
9	SAC Neil Chapman /© UK MOD Crown Copyright, 2011
10	Library of Congress, World War 1 Posters, LC-USZC4-10885
10	Library of Congress, World War 1 Posters, LC-USZC4-12697
10	© i4lcocl2 / Shutterstock.com, 85657522
11	Library of Congress, Miscellaneous items in high demand, LC-DIG-ppmsca-07629
12	LA(Phot) Paul A Barrow /© UK MOD Crown Copyright, 2005
13	Cpl Steve Bain ABIPP /© UK MOD Crown Copyright, 2009
14-15	POA(Phot) Sean Clee /© UK MOD Crown Copyright, 2006
16	© Elliot & Fry, Image: IWM (Q 69460)
17	Hugh Trenchard © IWM (Art.IWM ART 1829)
19	Library of Congress, War Paintings and Drawings by British Artists, LC-USZC4-10231
19	Library of Congress, World War 1 Posters, LC-USZC4-11295
19	Library of Congress, World War 1 Posters, LC-USZC4-11045
20	© Gary Blakeley, Shutterstock, 2323069
21	William George Barker © Image: IWM (Q 68086)
22	Albert Ball RFC © Birkett, Image: IWM (Q 69593)
22	The Last Fight of Captain Ball © IWM (Art.IWM ART 1488)
24	© Gary Blakeley, Shutterstock, 2323072
25	© Kletr, Shutterstock, 23387035
26	Alan Arnett McLeod, Personalities Collection, Archives of Manitoba, N480
27	Thomas Mottershead © Image: IWM (Q 58359)
28	Library of Congress, Miscellaneous German Photographs World War One, LC-USZ62-136103
29	© IWM (RAE-O 897)
29	© TSRL, en.wikipedia.org/wiki/File:504
29	© TSRL en.wikipedia.org/wiki/File:SE5A
31	Library of Congress, FSA/OWI Photograph Collection, LC-USW33-019093-C
32	Bomber Harris © IWM (TR 1093)
33	Poster © IWM (Art.IWM PST 3774)
34	© Neil Cousland, Shutterstock 28798597
36	© Neil Cousland, Shutterstock 10587634
39	Poster © IWM (Art.IWM PST 14629)
40	© IWM (CL 570)
40	George Thompson © IWM (CH 14685)
42-43	© Chris Jenner, Shutterstock, 57224110
45	Thomas Gray, © Saidman Illustrated © Image: IWM (HU 1235)
45	© Peter Baxter, Shutterstock, 5391037